Practise Being Godly

Colin Buchanan

Welcome to Practise Being Godly!

I've had a lot of fun making this book for you. Every page takes the truth from one of my songs and gives you things to do and read that will help you think about what God has to say to you through the Bible.

A grown up might like to sit and read this with you. After you've looked at each page, you can read a short verse or two from the Bible and pray together about what you've learnt. You might even like to read it with me by putting on the CD that comes with the book. There are a few of my other songs on the CD for you to enjoy, too. (All the songs in this book are from my CD called "Practise Being Godly".)

Oh, and one more thing! I have hidden Little Colin with his guitar all over the place.
Can you find him?

Colin

P.S. Special thanks for lots of hard work, help and encouragement
to my Chief Colour-in-er-er and good friend, Geoff R Thompson.

www.colinbuchanan.com.au

Practise Being Godly

What are some things that you like doing?
Singing? Kicking a ball? Drawing? Playing the guitar? Making things?
The more you do those things, the better you get at them. That's called practising. People practise sports and music and school work. The Bible says there's something that Christians are to practise most of all – practise being godly. That means that day by day, at home, at school, when we're playing or reading or whatever we're doing, we're to make God the centre of it. It means thanking Him and asking Him to help us obey. It means following Jesus by saying NO to sin and YES to God. I want to get better and better at doing that. Do you?

Who didn't practise?

Let's Pray

King Jesus, you are the ruler of all. Every good thing comes from you and everything was made to say, "Jesus is Great!" Forgive me for trusting in things that fade away and wanting glory for me instead of glory for you. Help me to show, in all I do, that peace with my precious Father God is the greatest treasure of all. Amen.

Build Your Life on the Rock

Jesus told a story about two men, each building a house. One built his house on the hard rock, the other guy built his house on the soft sand. Pitter patter! It started to rain. Splish splash! It rained and rained. Woosh! It rained so much that the water rose higher and higher and started to rush around the two houses. Creak...groan...SMASH! One house fell down! Which one do you think fell down? The house on the soft, shifting....sand! Which house stood up strong? The one built on the firm, strong, solid...rock! Jesus is the Rock.

If we build our lives on Him, if we obey Him, follow Him and trust Him, our lives will stand strong. Then when sickness, sadness, disappointment, tears, sin and even death come like a flood, we'll stand strong because He is strong. Will you build your life on Jesus? He's the Rock!

READ
THE BIBLE
Matthew
7:24–27

SING
*Build Your
Life on the
Rock*

Let's Pray

Lord Jesus, thank you that you are the Rock. Help me to build my life upon you. Show me when I am trusting in the things of this world. These things can't save me, they won't last. But sometimes these things take your place and that is wrong. I cannot put my hope on earthly things. Help me to trust in you alone, King Jesus. Amen.

He Died Upon the Cross

Did Jesus have to die on the cross? It was a very bad, very sad way to die. Many of Jesus' friends ran away or lied and said they never even knew Him. He was hurt and teased. When he was there, dying on the cross, His enemies made cruel fun of Him. They said, "If you're the Son of God, get down off the cross now and save yourself!" He could have, but He didn't. He cried out, "It is finished!" and he died. But it was God's plan to send Jesus to die to pay the price for sin and then to smash death to bits by rising from the grave. One day He's coming back to rule over ALL – FOREVER! God used Jesus' death on the bad, bad cross to break the power of dark, deadly sin and to bring good, good life to dead, dead sinners like you and me.

Chorus 'He died upon the cross'

Chorus 'He died upon the cross'

Chorus 'for'

Chorus 'me!'

Chorus 'One day when I was lost...'

Verse 2 'They laid Him in the grave...'

Verse 3 'He rose up from the dead...'

Verse 4 'He's coming back again...'

Everybody needs to be Saved

THE RICH

The POOR

The YOUNG

The OLD

The SMART

The SICK

THE HEALTHY

the STRONG

the SAD
sniff sniff

the HAPPY
Yippeee!

The GOOD
here you are...

VB 34 ME
I don't care
THE ONES WHO SAY THEY DON'T CARE

READ THE BIBLE
Romans 5:6–8

SING
He Died Upon the Cross

Let's Pray

O Jesus, thank you for obeying your Father and being obedient, even to death on the cross! I praise you because you smashed the power of sin and rose from the dead and will return in power to rule forever! Lord Jesus, you are the GREATEST! Amen.

Don't be Ashamed of the Lord

Let me tell you about Peter. We read about him in the Bible. He was a disciple, one of Jesus' close friends and followers. He once said to Jesus, "No matter what, I will always, always be your friend!" But only a little while later, when Jesus was taken away to be killed by bad men, Peter said to someone, "I never even knew Jesus!" He was scared and ashamed of Jesus. After he did that, he cried and cried. He knew he'd done a terrible thing to Jesus. But God did something special to Peter. He forgave Peter and showed him that Jesus rose from the dead. God gave Peter the Holy Spirit. After that, Peter wasn't scared or ashamed. He became a brave apostle – a fearless messenger for God. He wasn't scared of being hurt or thrown into prison or even killed for being Jesus' friend. He wasn't ashamed of the Lord any more. I pray that we will all be bold for God, like Peter.

Let's Pray

Jesus, thank you that you are a friend to the weak, the scared and the failures. I know I fail you. Thank you that you forgive all who believe in you. Thank you that the same Holy Spirit that changed Peter will change me as I follow you. Make me bold to say, "I follow Jesus! He is my King!" Amen.

Don't Bop 'em on the Head

I'll tell you a sad story about two brothers – one called Cain, the other called Abel. When they decided to bring a present to God, Abel brought meat and Cain brought fruit and vegetables. God was happy with Abel's present, but He wasn't happy with what Cain brought. Cain was so mad that he killed his brother Abel. What a sad, sad story. Jesus said that when we look at someone and our hearts are full of hatred, we're like Cain, the murderer – even if we don't actually do anything to them. Maybe we think about hurting them, or hope something bad happens to them. Of course, we might even start punching, biting, scratching or calling them names. But whether we do hurtful things or just think them, we sin against others and against God – like Cain did. Ask God to give you self-control and to make you not like Cain, the hater, but like Jesus, the Lover.

READ THE BIBLE Matthew 5:21–24

SING *Don't Bop 'em on the Head*

Let's Pray

O Jesus, it can be so hard to show self-control. Evil thoughts pop into my head so easily and all of a sudden I'm thinking wrong things and doing bad things. Jesus, help me to show self-control, to hate sin, to love and live your goodness. Amen.

Ephesians 2:8-10

Have you ever flown a kite? You hold the string and the wind blows the colourful kite up, up into the air. But...if you get too close to the trees, lookout! When your kite gets stuck in the trees it could get wrecked and that means no more flying. But...what if someone with a long ladder comes along and kindly and carefully untangles the kite, rolls up the string and gives it all back to you, safe and sound? Well, you could find a better place – away from the trees – to fly your kite again. Christians are saved from their sins – like that kite was untangled from the tree. Sin wrecks lives and we all need to be saved. Jesus carefully and kindly frees us from being wrecked forever by sin when we come to Him in faith.

But that's not the end of the story. The kite was freed to fly again, wasn't it? Only Jesus can save us from sin. Only Jesus can set us free to love and serve God and other people, just as God planned.

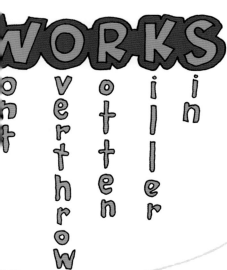

WORKS

o v o i i
h e t l n
t r t l
   t e e
   h n r
   r
   o
   w

GRACE

God's
Riches
At
Christ's
Expense

READ THE BIBLE
Ephesians 2:8–10

SING
Ephesians 2:8–10

CAN YOU...

PUTZ Cream of CARROT soup

Uh oh...

Run a car on soup?

Fly to the moon on a rocket made out of fish?

Teach a horse to build a TV set?

Y'all better hurry on there...

...the news is on at 6...

I hope the screen doesn't Flicka...

BITS

NO!

LIST OF GOOD WORKS
· went to church
· helped old lady
· prayed a lot
· gave money to poor

Be forgiven by God by doing good works?

🖐 *Let's Pray*

Dear God, it's so amazing that you save sinners! You are so full of goodness and mercy! I was helpless. I only deserved your holy anger, yet you saved me by the gift of faith in the Lord Jesus. Help me to use my freedom from sin to do the good things you have prepared for me to do. Amen.

I Can't Save Myself

What are you good at? Singing or dancing? Helping people, or making people happy? Playing sport or drawing? There are lots of things we do well. And there are things that none of us can do. We can't start or stop the rain, or jump over a mountain, or balance on one leg on a chair and hold an elephant on our finger. We say those things are impossible – none of us can do them! Everyone tries to get away from the badness of sin. We try to be nicer, we buy stuff and do things to make us feel better for a little while. We treasure all sorts of stuff instead of treasuring and believing in Jesus.

How can we be saved when sin's badness is on the inside of us as well as the outside? Only one person can save us from dark and deadly sin. Not you. Not me. Who? Jesus! No matter how I try, I can't save myself!

Some things Colin (and you) CAN'T DO...

Kiss his own elbow!

Balance on a chair on one leg while holding an elephant on his finger...

Drink all the water in the Tasman Sea!

ooo urgh!!

Weeeee!

Jump over a mountain

Lift himself off the ground.

Hrrrrr!

STOP! Welcome to Sunny CAIRNS GO!

Stand in Cairns and stop the rain.

✗ Christians aren't saved BY good works

I CAN'T SAVE MYSELF   JESUS SAVES!

✓ Christians are saved FOR good works

READ THE BIBLE
Acts 4:12

SING
I Can't Save Myself

Let's Pray

Great and Mighty Lord, you are the God who saves!
Every person is born under the curse of sin and death and is an enemy of you.
Thank you that you made a way of escaping your judgement. I could never
do that, but Jesus did! Thank you, Holy Saviour! Amen.

John 1:1

Words are very useful, aren't they? We use them to tell people what we need, how we feel and what we're thinking. Words answer our questions and tell us what we need to know. With words, we can make friends and talk together. There are lots of words in this book. Can you point to one? Now, can you say your name? Even your name is a word.

One of the names the Bible gives Jesus is, "The Word." That's an unusual name, isn't it? Why do you think God would call Him that? Jesus was called "The Word" because God spoke to us through Him. Jesus is God. He has always been there and always will be. When God became a man – first a baby, then a boy, then a grown up – everything He said and everything He did told us what God is like.

No one can know God without coming to Jesus – God's Living Word!

JESUS is ETERNAL
He has ALWAYS been there and ALWAYS will be!
COLOSSIANS 1:17   REVELATION 11:15

Things that haven't always been there (and won't be there one day.)

Phil's new boat

The Sydney Opera House

The pyramids

Priceless works of art

MONA LISA
NOT FOR SALE

lovely old buildings!

Ye OFFICIAL LOVELY OLDE BUILDING King Henry passed by (we think)

DONG! DONG! DONG!

Big Ben (a very BIG, very OLD clock)

prizes

GOLDEN CHEESE AWARDS

WINNER

READ
THE BIBLE
John
1:1-5;14

SING
John 1:1

Let's Pray

Lord, thank you that you are a God who speaks. Thank you that your Words are words of truth, forgiveness and life! Thank you that Jesus is the Living Word of God. Through Him you speak good, good news for sinners who will believe in Him. Help me to listen to Jesus and obey all He says. Amen.

Let Your Light Shine

Close your eyes and tell me, what do you see? Nothing – just blackness, like night time. When the sun has gone and there's no moon it can be very hard to see anything. But what if you turn on a light or someone holds up a candle? Suddenly you can see where it's safe to walk, without tripping over or bumping into or breaking things. I'd much rather be in the light than in the dark, wouldn't you? Jesus called Himself the Light of the world. He shines love and hope and forgiveness into the dark, hopeless, sinful world. And he said that if we follow Him, we can shine His light, too. The way God's children live and what they say can help people in the darkness look to Jesus – the Light of the World. So if you love Jesus, let your light shine!

...Let your LIGHT shine before men, that they may see your GOOD DEEDS and praise your FATHER in heaven.

Point to the things that give Light

READ
THE BIBLE
Matthew
5:14–16

SING
Let
Your Light
Shine

Let's Pray

O God, there is so much darkness in the world. Sin brings blackness and sadness and death. Thank you that you shine into the darkness. Jesus, you are the Light of the World. Help me to shine for you, to live in the light and show others that you are the only way out of the darkness. Amen.

Little by Little

Some things move very, very slowly, don't they? A snail sliding along the ground takes a long time to get anywhere. The hands of a clock are always moving, but you need to look very closely to see them move. The earth is always moving, going from day to night and back to day, but we don't see it moving. Slow things can seem to be standing still. But when you come back, the snail is gone, the clock has changed, the sun has gone down. God is changing His children to be more like Jesus, but sometimes it can feel to them like it's happening very slowly. However day-by-day, He's helping them to love self and sin less and love and serve Him and others more and more. It may seem as if you're growing like Jesus verrrry slowly, but if you've trusted Him, God's Holy Spirit is changing you – little by little, everyday.

Are these things Slow or FAST?

READ THE BIBLE
orinthians 3:16
Philippians 3:20–21

SING
Little by Little

Let's Pray

Lord God, thank you that you promise to change your children to make them more and more like the Lord Jesus. Help me to say no to sin and yes to you. Thank you that one day I will see you and sin will be gone forever. Please keep showing me the things you want me to change and give me your power to be more like Jesus. Amen.

Luke 9:23

Have you ever played follow the leader? Someone is the leader and everyone else has to go where the leader goes and do what they say. If they hop, you hop. If they sing, "La la laaaa!" you have to sing, "La la laaaa!" If they tiptoe, or skip, or jump, you do the same. Jesus said that if we're His friends, we'll do just what He says and live like He lived. The good things He did weren't always easy things. As a follower of Jesus you may have to miss out on some things. You may see other people enjoying something that you think you deserve – but following Jesus means he is your number one. Sometimes it will be very, very hard, just like it was very, very hard for Jesus to obey His Father and go to the cross to die. There will be hard, sad, difficult times for Jesus' followers – but the sad times won't last forever!

Can you follow the ants and find the honey?

Follow the leader...
Point to them and do what they're doing...

whistle

Yeah! Yeah! Yeah!

dance!

Ha Ha Ha — laugh

stand on one leg

Z z z z z z z — go to sleep

clap your hands

singing — La / La laaa!

cry... Boo hoo

Yay! I found the honey!

READ THE BIBLE
Luke 9:22–25

SING
Luke 9:23

Let's Pray

O Jesus, help me to follow you. Thank you that you are strong and even if I am weak, or sad, or very tired, I can follow you. I want to leave behind sin and pride to follow you and be like you, serving and loving and seeking God's glory. Lead me, Lord Jesus! Amen.

Mighty to Save

Have you ever seen a rescue? Perhaps you've seen firefighters rescue someone from a burning building. Or a lifesaver at the beach dive out through the waves and drag a struggling swimmer to safety. People in trouble need a rescuer – someone strong and willing and brave enough to save them. We all need to be saved from sin. Sin is deadly. We can't save ourselves. That's why we need someone who is mighty and kind and willing to save us from our sin. Is there anyone who would or could do that? Only one – Jesus! He alone was brave enough to die for us, good enough to rise from the dead, mighty enough to save us. How wonderful to call on Him and know He will rescue us. He will keep us safely in His care – forever! Have you been saved?

People in the Bible who were saved.

Daniel in the lion's den.

The Israelites in Egypt

SNAP!

The demon-possessed man of the tombs

Praise ye the LORD!

Peter and John in prison

THWAK!

David from bad King Saul

"...but I call to GOD and the LORD saves me..."
Psalm 55:16

Match the RESCUERS with ones who need RESCUING.

RESCUE

READ
THE BIBLE
[Ze]phaniah 3:17
Colossians
1:13–14

SING
Mighty to Save

Let's Pray

Jesus, you are such a great and mighty Saviour! No one else could save me from judgement, sin and death! Thank you for being faithful to your Father in heaven, all the way to the cross. Thank you for opening the way to life for all who turn from sin and call on you to save them. Amen.

More Like Jesus

Who do you look like? Do people say that you look like your mum or dad? Perhaps sometimes you dress up and pretend you're a nurse, a police officer, a super hero or a cowboy. We all look at other people sometimes and think, "I'd like to be like them!" But most of all we should want to be like Jesus! Jesus was the best, most wonderful man that ever lived. He never ever did anything wrong – never! Not even one secret, tiny sin! Wow! Could you or I ever be like that? Well, God promises something wonderful to everyone who believes in Jesus. He promises that their sins are forgiven and that one day they really will be like Jesus. And day-by-day, He helps them to become more like Jesus in the way they love and live and serve. If you're forgiven, ask God to make you more like Jesus – every day!

For those God foreknew He also predestined to be conformed to the likeness of His Son...
Romans 8:29

Who are they, trying to be like?

What makes what?
Can you match them up?

READ THE BIBLE
Ephesians 5:1–2

SING
More Like Jesus

Let's Pray

O Jesus, there could be nothing better than becoming more like you. Like you in loving your Father, like you in loving other people, like you in the way I live and think and speak. Mighty God, will you please make me more like Jesus in every way? Amen.

The Greatest Treasure

A treasure is something precious, something that is very, very special to you. People have lots of different treasures. It might be stuff like money, jewels, gold, houses, toys or cars. Other people treasure friends, family or being famous. Some want to be loved by lots of people or win all the time. Are these things treasures that will never end? No! Robbers steal stuff. Things get burned and wrecked. Winners stop winning. People can stop liking you. And death can take family and friends away. But there's a treasure that will never, ever end – even after you die. What's the greatest treasure in the whole wide world? Peace with God! Everyone who has peace with God through Jesus has been given a treasure that will never, ever fade. What a precious gift from God!

where be the treasure chests?

How many treasure chests can you find in the picture?

READ THE BIBLE James 1:10–12

SING *The Greatest Treasure*

Let's Pray

Lord God, you created me to show how great and wonderful you are. Please give me your power to say no to sin and centre all I do on you. No matter where I am, may I live like there is nothing more important than God and His ways. You see and know my every moment – help me to live each one for you. Amen

Here are the words
of the songs featured
in this book.

Practise Being Godly

1. Have you seen those fit and healthy
   guys,
   Always doin' their exercise?
   Well it's better to work for a
   heavenly prize,
   So practise being godly.

   CHORUS
   Never give up, make it your aim.
   Practise being godly.
   If you've been forgiven in Jesus' name,
   Practise being godly.
   He paid the price for all our sin,
   His Holy Spirit dwells within,
   So centre all you do on him...
   Practise being godly.

2. You can lift big weights, you can
   swim or run,
   Train everyday to be number one,
   But it's better to train for the life
   to come.
   Practise being godly.

3. Well, walk with the Lord wherever
   you go.
   Whatever you're doing, he will know.
   Say, 'Yes! to God'.
   To sin say, 'No'!
   Practise being godly.

Words and Music by Colin Buchanan
© 1997 Rondor Music (Aust)

Mighty To Save

1. Oh Lord, my God, I cry to you for
   mercy,
   And you heard me.
   Oh Lord, my God,
   You rescued me from the grave...
   CHORUS
   And you are mighty.
   The Lord is mighty.
   He is mighty.
   Call to the Lord, for he is mighty
   to save.

2. Oh Lord, my God, I cry to you for
   help,
   And you heal me.
   Oh Lord, my God,
   You wash me whiter than snow...

   CHORUS

   BRIDGE
   He turned my mourning to dancing,
   Sorrow to joy,
   Silence to singing,
   And I will praise his name for evermore.

   Repeat verse 1

Words and Music by Colin Buchanan
© 1997 Rondor Music (Aust)

Luke 9:23

Then Jesus said ... two, three, four:
'If anyone would come, come after me,
If anyone would come, come after me,
He must deny himself
And take his cross up daily
And follow, follow, follow, follow,
Follow, follow, follow me.'
That's Luke chapter nine, verse twenty
three.

Words and Music by Colin Buchanan
© 1997 Rondor Music (Aust)

The Greatest Treasure

Well the greatest treasure
in the whole wide world is
Peace with God.
Yeah, the greatest treasure
in the whole wide world is
Peace with God.
It's the only treasure that will never fade.
Even death can't take it away.
Yeah, the greatest treasure
in the whole wide world is
Peace with God.

1. You can live for happiness, or live
   for stuff
   But it's all going to fade away.
   But you'll never, ever feel like
   you've got enough
   Because it's all going to fade away.
   The trickiest toys that money can buy
   Are all going to fade away,
   Because the greatest treasure...

2. What if the world makes you a
   star?
   It's all going to fade away.
   The biggest house and the flashiest
   car!
   They're all going to fade away.
   Earthly treasures like the morning
   mist
   Are all going to fade away.

Because the greatest treasure
in the whole wide world is
Peace with God.
Yeah, the greatest treasure
in the whole wide world is
Peace with God.

It's the only treasure that will never fade.
Even death can't take it away.
Yeah, the greatest treasure
in the whole wide world is
Peace with God.

Words and Music by Colin Buchanan
© 1997 Rondor Music (Aust)

John 1:1

'In the beginning
In the beginning
Was the Word, and Word was God.'

'In the beginning
In the beginning
Was the Word, and Word was God.'

John, chapter one,
John, chapter one,
John, chapter one, verse one.

Words and Music by Colin Buchanan
© 1997 Rondor Music (Aust)

I Can't Save Myself

1. I can't drink all the water in the
   Tasman Sea.
   I'll never be as tall as an old gum tree.
   I can't count all the yabbies in
   Cooper's Creek
   And I can't save myself.

   CHORUS
   Just when I was powerless,
   Helpless in my sin,
   Jesus won forgiveness,
   So I could be born again.
   I had no choice, I came to him,
   'Cause I can't save myself.

2. I can't stop all the sunshine
   on the Nullarbor Plain.
   I can't stand in Cairns and stop
   the rain.
   I can't catch all the mullet in the
   River MacLean
   And I can't save myself.

3. I'll never catch all the bunnies
   on the Darling Downs.
   I'll never move the Olgas into town
   Can't make a flock of Cockies
   keep the noise down
   And I can't save myself.

Words and Music by Colin Buchanan
© 1997 Rondor Music (Aust)

Ephesians 2:8-10

Ephesians, chapter two, verse eight
to ten.
Ephesians, chapter two, verse eight
to ten.
'For it is by grace you have been
saved
And not by works so nobody can
boast,
For we are God's workmanship
Created for Wo, oh, oh!

Words and Music by Colin Buchanan
© 1997 Rondor Music (Aust)

Don't Be Ashamed O
The Lord

1. I can make you feel like a loony-
   tune,
   Like a total goose, like a big baboon.
   One day they will change their tune
   So don't be ashamed of the Lord.

   CHORUS
   Nothing anyone can say or do
   Will change who God is
   And what he's done for you
   What's right is right,
   What's true is true
   So don't be ashamed of the Lord,
   no, no, no
   Don't be ashamed of the Lord.

2. I might say you're a few cents
   short of a quid,
   You've lost you're marbles,
   That you've flipped your lid.
   But that won't change what Jesus
   did,
   So don't be ashamed of the Lord.

3. I might say your sick,
   And you're looking pale,
   That your God, well he's surely failed,
   Like Paul, you might end up in jail, hey
   Don't be afraid of the Lord

Let Your Light Shine

CHORUS
Let your light shine, let it be seen.
Let everybody see your love.
Let you light shine, let it be seen,
To the praise of the mighty God above.

1. When you're feeling happy,
   When you're feeling sad,
   When things go well or when things
   go bad...

   CHORUS

2. In the way you speak
   And in what you do
   Others might see the Lord in you...

   CHORUS

More Like Jesus

1. He was his Father's faithful Son.
   His love for God, it was number
   one.
   He lived the truth every single day.
   Lord, I want to love you that way.

   CHORUS
   More like Jesus,
   More like him.
   Ask the Lord to make you more like
   Jesus.

2. He loved the outcast and the
   despised,
   Spoke the truth without
   compromise.
   He ached for a world that groaned
   in sin.
   Lord, I want to be just like him.

   CHORUS

3. He faced the anger of his enemies.
   His God was who he lived to please.
   He took up the cross in his Father's
   name.
   If we follow Christ, we're to do
   the same.

   CHORUS

Don't Bop 'em on the Head

1. I know that there's a golden rule,
   'Don't get back' and 'don't be cruel',
   'Use self control' and 'keep your cool'.
   I learnt it all in Grundy school.
   It goes like this ...

   CHORUS
   Don't bop 'em on the head.
   Don't kick 'em and yank their hair.
   Don't punch and bite and scratch
   and call them names.
   'Cause if you go the dummy-spit
   The Lord will not be pleased with it.
   It's not so weak to turn the other
   cheek.

2. But you-know-who, he stands in
   line
   And pushes in every time.
   I get so mad, 'cause I was first
   And once or twice, I've yelled
   and cursed...

3. But one day, I had chockie cake
   For little lunch at morning break
   And you-know-who, he punched
   it hurt
   And all my cake plopped in the
   dirt...

4. I think that I begin to see
   No matter what is done to me
   I've got to think and make my goal
   To STOP!
   And show some self control...
   AAAAAANNNNNDDDDDD...

   CHORUS

Little By Little

CHORUS
Little by little everyday,
Little by little in every way,
Jesus is changing me.
Since I've made that turn-about-face,
I've been growing in his grace.
Jesus is changing me.
He's changing me,
My precious Saviour.
I'm not the same person that I used
to be.
Well, its been slow going
But there's a knowing
That someday, perfect I will
Someday, perfect I will
Someday perfect I will be.

Build Your Life On The Rock

1. Well two men, were their houses
   a-building,
   One on rock and one built on the sand.
   When the floods washed around
   One just fell to the ground,
   But that house on the rock, it did stand.

   CHORUS
   Build your life on the rock, and it's Jesus.
   Put your hope on the Lord's living word.
   It's the only solid ground
   That will not let you down.
   Build your life, put your hope on the rock.

2. If you're living for fame and for money,
   Well you're digging yourself one big
   hole,
   'Cause treasure on earth
   Has no lasting worth.
   There's no gain in losing your soul.

3. Trust in Jesus and seek first his
   kingdom.
   Seek his honour and strive to obey.
   Give your heart and your soul
   To your heavenly goal
   That won't perish, that won't fade away.

He Died Upon The Cross

1. He died upon the cross.
   He died upon the cross.
   He died upon the cross
   For me, for me, for just for me.

   CHORUS
   One day when I was lost
   He died upon the cross.
   He died upon the cross
   For me, for me, for just for me.

2. They laid him in the grave...

3. He rose up from the dead...

4. He's coming back again...

These songs are all from my CD, 'Practise Being Godly', which is available separately

Can you match the **picture** to the **commandment?**

1. You shall have NO other gods before me.
2. You shall not make an idol and bow down and worship it.
3. You shall not misuse the name of the LORD your God.
4. Remember the Sabbath day by keeping it holy.
5. Honour your father and mother.
6. You shall not murder.
7. You shall not commit adultery.
8. You shall not steal.
9. You shall not lie.
10. You shall not covet anything that belongs to someone else.

DONG! DONG! DONG!

MONA LISA
NOT FOR SALE